"Great book if you are thinking about starting a business."

Daniel Priestley
Author of 'Key Person of Influence' and 'Entrepreneur Revolution'

I'M AN ENTREPRENEUR - GET ME OUT OF HERE!

THE LESSONS

Entrepreneurial insight for those who haven't the time to faff around.

BAIJU SOLANKI

All rights reserved. No part of this publication may be reproduced, stored in a retrieval system or transmitted in any form or by any means, electronic, mechanical, photocopying or otherwise, without the prior written permission of the publisher.

Published in 2014 by CreateSpace Independent Publishing Platform

© 2014 Baiju Solanki

ISBN 978 1 4959312 5 3

Editorial, interior design and typesetting by Callisto Green
www.callistogreen.com

Cover Design by The Grow Creative Company www.justgrow.co

Acknowledegments

This is my first book and it has been a long time coming. Nothing would have been possible without the support and love of my wife Sangita. When I wanted to leave the security of a full-time job to pursue my own entrepreneurial journey, she was supportive all the way. I want to also thank my children, Sapna, Milan and Suraj, for always making me laugh even when things didn't seem too funny.

I would like to thank all those entrepreneurs who took the time out of their business schedules to be interviewed for this book.

Publishing a book is about more than creating the content. I would like to thank Vicki Watson for her patience and advice while creating and editing this book, and Rich With for his design insights. In addition I would like to acknowledge Warren Cass, for putting a little seed of inspiration in my head that was the ultimate catalyst for this book.

Finally, since leaving my job there have been many people who have helped me along the way; too many to mention them all. Many of them have been interviewed for this book. I choose these people because in one way or another they have influenced the way I do business. Also my parents and extended family have all in their unique way given me the inspiration to follow my dreams and help others follow theirs. Thank you.

'Entrepreneurship is not for the faint of heart. It's not for the timid of mind. It's not for the wildly expectacious. It's not for the easily bothered and swayed. It's not for the non-action takers. It's not for the 'freebie seekers' and it's most definitely not for those who dwell on problems.

It IS for...the bold. The courageous. Those who get over their problems quicker then they dwell on them. Those who change their thinking the second the moment calls for it. Those who are willing to give up everything, no matter what is being asked. Those who care more about creating something beautiful than potentially losing something beautiful. It's for those who simply don't know any other way to be than ENTREPRENEURIAL...and they're willing to give it their ALL, even if it's the last they've got to give.'

'The best reason to start an organisation is to make meaning — to create a product or service to make the world a better place.'

Jonathan Budd

Contents

Section 1 – Introduction 7

Section 2 – The Lessons 19

Five Lessons from Daniel 22

Five Lessons from David 26

Five Lessons from Steve 30

Five Lessons from Chris 34

Five Lessons from Thomas 38

Five Lessons from Suraj 42

Five Lessons from Vicki 46

Five Lessons from Simon 50

Five Lessons from Sue 54

Five Lessons from Penny 58

Five Lessons from Brad 62

Section 3 – Conclusion 65

Summary of Lessons 71

This book is dedicated to everybody who has an entrepreneurial spirit. This spirit is often manifested in money-making ventures. However the entrepreneurial drive can develop through social enterprise, charities, the younger generation, and even communities. Whatever it is you love doing, you can find a way to make it happen and make a living. This book is for you.

Section 1

Introduction

What is entrepreneurship?

The common definition of an entrepreneur is, "One who undertakes innovations, finances and business acumen in an effort to transform innovations into economic goods." Or in layman's terms, someone who starts a project or business to make money.

But whilst the end goal might be financial, it has been shown that entrepreneurship is much more than that, and is actually about creating something where money and wealth is the yardstick by which success is measured.

The public image of the entrepreneur, epitomized by *'Dragon's Den'* or *'The Apprentice'*, is of a highly motivated and determined individual with an ego the size of Mars. Yet this is not always the case; in fact it is seldom so. Entrepreneurs come in all shapes and sizes.

There have been numerous debates about whether entrepreneurs are born or made. To come to any conclusion, the first things to establish are the key characteristics of an entrepreneur.

One of the core behaviours of an entrepreneur is their willingness to take on risk. Any kind of risk? No. The entrepreneur takes calculated risks, risks that have a higher chance of return if the appropriate amount of planning and research is done. Entrepreneurship also has a lot to do with gut feeling, intuition and doing what feels right.

There is a tendency to look at the logical and measurable characteristics of what makes a good entrepreneur, yet if you look at just the logical and the traits that can be measured in a spreadsheet, you won't find an entrepreneur but a manager. Entrepreneurship is not a job, but a way of life.

So when an entrepreneur evaluates risk, they tend to think not of what could go wrong but what could go right; their cup is usually half full. This positive mental attitude gives the entrepreneur greater confidence, which in itself opens their mind to further ideas and possibilities, triggering exponential growth.

Another entrepreneurial characteristic is that of grasping opportunities. Entrepreneurs have an innate tendency to not only seek out but be presented with opportunities that others can only wish for. But is this really the case? It could be argued that opportunities are available all the time to all people, but that most people have their eyes closed and don't notice what's around them. When you purchase a new car, for example, do you tend to notice that that make and model of car seems to be everywhere?! Did everyone suddenly buy the same car or are you now more conscious about it and hence notice them more? They were always there, of course – it's just that back then they weren't on your radar.

Entrepreneurs are more open to ideas and are always consciously and subconsciously looking for opportunities. You might argue that it is not that most people don't see opportunities, but that they don't have the resources to take them. Yet the way in which an entrepreneur thinks is not in terms of what resources they need, but rather of how resourceful they can become with what they already have. This is a completely different way of thinking, and one that time and again distinguishes entrepreneurs from employees.

Another trait that may not be immediately obvious but in fact proves essential is discipline. When an entrepreneur has an idea and vision, they need to take appropriate action to make it happen. Of course, not everything will turn out as they planned and they will get frustrated. This is where discipline is so important. When you are building your business, you need to have the discipline to work on the dull, less-than-interesting parts and work unsociable hours. As an entrepreneur, you are top of the tree and have no one to keep you on track. Many highly successful entrepreneurs have a coach or mentor for this very reason.

Entrepreneurship brings out traits in people that they never knew they had. When you talk to entrepreneurs who are about to embark on their journey, they have a belief that their service/product is so good that this in itself will get them through the tough times of growing their business. Once on their journey, they realise that they need to have a determination to succeed that goes way beyond anything else they have done before.

You see, as an entrepreneur, it's not about the pay-cheque. You are not guaranteed a lump sum of money at the end of the each month. When you are running your own enterprise, there could be many months before any money comes in at all and longer still before you can pay yourself. To truly succeed, in addition to providing an outstanding service or product, you also need:

- Self-belief
- Determination to succeed
- Unwavering commitment
- Persistence to achieve great things
- The ability to embrace hard work
- The ability to accept responsibility

And above all, the ability to enjoy the work you are doing.

The money will come in time, but it is the above things, together with a focused mind, that will ensure you become the entrepreneur you want to be.

So why become an entrepreneur?

There's no better time than now to become an entrepreneur. Why? Because in today's society, everybody can easily access the tools they need and the barrier or entry is so low. We are living in the Entrepreneurial Revolution. In fact, Daniel Priestley, one of the entrepreneurs interviewed in this book, talks about this being the Age of the Entrepreneur.

But this isn't the first time the Entrepreneurial Revolution has been upon us. In the 1800s, before the Industrial Revolution, entrepreneurs abounded; farmers, bakers, butchers. Then the Industrial Revolution brought us factories and people moved away from rural areas into cities, setting the tone for the 9-5 lifestyle. It was from these times that we started to get conditioned into working for big corporations and factories and became accustomed to the idea of exchanging our time for money. But like everything, nothing is permanent and the

Internet, amongst other technological advances, has enabled the Entrepreneurial Revolution to re-emerge.

Since the late 1900s, we have been conditioned into the mindset of getting a good education and working hard to earn every penny. We learn that this is the way it is and the way it is always going to be. Although the idea of wealth creation has always been around, we are led to believe that it is only available to the select few; the rest of us will remain slaves to the 9-5 working lifestyle.

So why become an entrepreneur? Put simply, because you can! Now don't get me wrong, entrepreneurship is not for everyone. I know plenty of people who don't mind – or even love – the security that their 9-5 job gives them. They are prepared to exchange their time for working to someone else's agenda for five days of the week in order to have the weekend to themselves. They are happy to do this until they retire and there is nothing wrong with that.

However, what is happening more and more now is that people who are slaves to the 9-5 are starting to complain that they can't start their own business or follow their passion because they have responsibilities, a mortgage, kids, bills…and so the list goes on. This is a little like saying that they would rather suffer years of dull pain than a few years or even months of acute pain, to live the life they want. Crazy.

But coming back to the question, 'Why become an entrepreneur?', never before in our recent history have the resources, opportunities and environment been more conducive to starting a business. The 'job for life' is no longer an option, the pension pots are dwindling, we are living far longer than our predecessors and we cannot rely upon the state to look after us. The only way to be able to sustain the kind of lifestyle we dream of, not only during our working lives but well into our retirement too, is to create our own wealth through the opportunity of entrepreneurship.

Choice. You still have a choice. If you want the security a job gives, you can do that; if you want to follow the entrepreneurial path, you can do that too – it's just a matter of choice. Years ago, in order to start a business you would have needed finance, staff, premises and infrastructure. Today all you need is a laptop, a phone, an idea and some good old-fashioned determination!

Don't make the assumption that this is a young man's game and that if you are the wrong side of 40 you cannot start your own business. In some cases you may actually be at an advantage. Life teaches us lessons, and the world we live in requires transferable skills. Applying skills learned in one domain to a new one gives you an edge, one which you cannot learn in the classroom.

Entrepreneurship is always been about being resourceful with what you have rather than having resources, but with the advent of the Internet, technological advances, social media and also the acceptance of people following their dreams and passions, starting a business has become easier. This doesn't mean it is easier to run or to make successful, but just that the barriers to starting a business have never been lower.

If you are still unsure of whether you should or even could be an entrepreneur, respond to these statements with either Yes or No:

- ☑ I don't like being told what to do.
- ☑ I like to lead, not follow.
- ☑ I like to have variety in my life.

- ☑ I'm not scared of failure.
- ☑ I like taking calculated risks.
- ☑ I love challenges that stretch me.
- ☑ I find it easy to delegate tasks.
- ☑ I hate routine.
- ☑ When I am doing work I like, time is not an issue.
- ☑ When I work for someone else, I am always thinking of ways I would change things.
- ☑ I believe that nothing is impossible if you put your mind to it.
- ☑ I don't take no for an answer.
- ☑ I know the only way to create true wealth is to run my own business.
- ☑ I have dreams I want to pursue.
- ☑ There are no problems, only opportunities.
- ☑ If you answered yes to twelve or more, you are ready to become an entrepreneur!

Why I wrote this book

I am not a natural businessman, if there is such a thing. I started in academia and my first job was as a Psychology Lecturer at a college. I loved my job, working with people who wanted to learn about human behaviour. During this time I actually wanted to go and teach at a university, so enrolled on a part-time Master's course in Sports Science, majoring in Psychology. I did this whilst teaching full-time.

To complete my final dissertation, I left my teaching position as it was becoming too demanding. I still needed to earn a living but didn't want a career-changing job or anything too taxing. So I thought Sales would be good.

Fortunately for me, I found a Sales job that involved talking to and working with academic institutions. This suited me, as I talked their language. My aim was to be there for only six months or so, until I had finished my Master's degree.

I had never sold anything before and didn't really know anything about selling. If truth be told, I taught myself. The training provided involved half a day of products knowledge and learning which people I should be talking to. Thereafter I was left virtually on my own. Looking back now, I think that part of this was due to the fact that I had worked in a college and already knew the inside workings. It was really just about asking questions, which is what Sales is all about – a little like entrepreneurship and starting a business, not that I knew that then.

Six months on, I got my Master's and was ready to apply to universities. But something was happening – I was selling and quite enjoying it. In the first six months I had been promoted to Team Leader. Knowing how sales works now, this wasn't really much, but at the time I thought it was fantastic. Additionally, I was earning good money – more money in six months than I had earned in a year teaching. So I decided to stay in Sales, my thinking being, 'I will carry on for a bit whilst I am doing well and if and when it goes pear-shaped, I always have my Master's and can go and teach at any time.'

After nine years, thousands of air-miles, hundreds of sales and numerous promotions, I had reached the dizzy heights of Sales Director. Nine months into the job, I discovered coaching and this is when the next stage of my journey started. For five or six years I talked a lot about what I was going to do and went to many free and paid seminars about starting your business, making your next millions, the next big Internet thing… everything and anything.

The most valuable lesson from this was, however, not the 'stuff' I learnt, but simply talking to people who were starting their own business and hearing about the challenges they were facing.

Yes, we have all seen *'Dragons' Den'* and other business programs. One part of me looked at these highly successful entrepreneurs and thought, 'Wow, I want to be that successful.' The other part of me looked at them and thought, 'I can't really relate to them. They are too far away, in terms of finance, lifestyle, availability, even celebrity. They're not like me.'

I decided that I wanted to give people an insight into being an entrepreneur through entrepreneurs they could relate to, people who had started their business in the last five years or so. When you hear these people talk, the challenges you face become more real and manageable. So why only entrepreneurs who have started their businesses so recently? Simply because the rules of engagement have changed so dramatically over this period of time.

Between the late 1990s and about 2005, business was more or less the same, in that the method of getting customers and marketing was quite traditional, involving cold-calling, advertisements, PR, direct mail and so on. From the mid- to the late noughties, the rules changed dramatically and whatever their service or product, entrepreneurs have had to adapt to the changing market of Internet, social media and networking.

The reasons for people doing business with certain other people have, of course, never changed – we do business with people we know, like and trust – but the methods employed have evolved. Now it is possible to get to know someone without ever meeting them. You can grow to like them with the value they give online and trust is built through online referrals and recommendations.

I finally made the decision to leave my job in 2006, although didn't actually leave until the end of 2007. I used the year and a half between making the decision and actually leaving to get myself into a position to leave on my terms, as well as in saving enough money to survive for a year without any income. From speaking to others, the consensus seemed to be that when you leave a salaried job to start your own business, you should be prepared for a full year without any income. The stories in this book include some great examples of what other entrepreneurs did before they took an income.

Since leaving my job five years ago, I have not only started my training and coaching business, but have had the opportunity to be a partner in a restaurant, Saffron Lounge, and also been part of a highly successful health and fat-loss program called the Ultimate Body Transformation Blueprint.

Throughout this book, our eleven entrepreneurs give their insights not only on the practical issues they confronted, but the personal ones too. This book highlighted the five lessons that each of us can learn from the interviews given by the eleven entrepreneurs in my first book, *I'm an Entrepreneur – Get Me Out of Here!* In addition, each entrepreneur has given three key tips for budding entrepreneurs.

This pocket book is just the start – the start of my passion to help others follow their dreams and create the lives they want.

I hope you find the stories andn tips here an inspiration to start your business.

Who this book is for

This book is aimed at two types of individual. Perhaps you are sitting in your office now thinking, 'I would love to start my own business but I don't know how.' You may have children, a mortgage and bills to pay and simply can't see a realistic way of leaving your job to launch your own business. If so, this book is for you. The lessons you will read here are certain to enthuse, motivate and inspire you to take those first steps, providing you with succinct lessons and tips from people who have been there and done it themselves.

Or maybe you've already made the jump and started your own business. If so, congratulations! This book is for you too. The start-up stage of any business abounds with challenges and obstacles. If you're still in the early stages, wondering why it's so hard, why you're working harder, working longer hours and earning less money than before, this book can help. With jargon-free advice on networking, building teams, finance, marketing and social media, you will be confident and well-equipped to get your business through those difficult early stages and well on the way to becoming a flourishing, fulfilling and profitable venture.

Each of the eleven entrepreneurs in this book are real people. Some have been through bankruptcy and others have worked in the corporate world. Some have had a vision about their business for a lifetime, whilst others found their entrepreneurial path later on in life. But all of them made the decision to begin their own entrepreneurial journey and had the tenacity to follow it through. Overcoming barriers and resistance, they are now successful entrepreneurs and reaping the rewards of their hard work.

Section 2

The Lessons

'Our deepest fear is not that we are inadequate. Our deepest fear is that we are powerful beyond measure. It is our light, not our darkness that most frightens us. We ask ourselves, Who am I to be brilliant, gorgeous, talented, and fabulous? Actually, who are you not to be? You are a child of God. Your playing small does not serve the world. There is nothing enlightened about shrinking so that other people will not feel insecure around you.

We are all meant to shine, as children do. We were born to make manifest the glory of God that is within us. It is not just in some of us; it is in everyone and as we let our own light shine, we unconsciously give others permission to do the same. As we are liberated from our own fear, our presence automatically liberates others.'

Marianne Williamson

I'm an Entrepreneur - Get Me Out of Here! The Lessons

Daniel Priestley

> 'The best reason to start an organisation is to make meaning – to create a product or service to make the world a better place.'
>
> Guy Kawasaki

Daniel Priestley, the co-founder of Entrevo Ltd is a successful entrepreneur, international speaker and author of the bestselling books *'Become a Key Person of Influence'* and *'The Entrepreneur Revolution'*.

Daniel is passionate about helping business owners and entrepreneurs become a key person of influence in their industry through Entrevo's training programmes which are in the US, UK, Singapore and Australia. For more information please see www.keypersonofinfluence.com.

Five Lessons from Daniel

Lesson 1 – Leverage

Daniel was very clear in what he wanted to do – build an events company, similar to what he had done in Australia. Lesson within a lesson here: stick to what you are good at and don't try to be and do everything.

Daniel identified very quickly that to get his vision off the ground he needed to speak to a lot of the right people quickly. When you want to attract people to an event, the conventional thinking is to go directly to your target audience. What Daniel did was look to identify influential people who were already speaking to his audience and set up joint ventures and collaborations.

He set up a dinner party and leveraged others people's contacts with a win-win-win scenario, where he wins, the partner wins and the audience wins as they get news of an event from a trusted source.

Lesson 2 – Take care of the little things

When we start a business, we correctly focus on the big things that need to be done, such as meeting clients and preparing products and services, but don't underestimate the little things that need attention in order to get your business going. Coming from another country, one of Daniel's frustrations was getting a mobile phone and bank accounts sorted out. Be aware of these things and very quickly look to delegate the little things that need to be done but that don't necessarily meet your flow.

Lesson 3 - Make it about the customer

When Daniel came to the UK, he had a vision to build an events company that would be recognized as one of the best, if not the best, in the UK. Why? To make money, to build a legacy, to meet a challenge and probably all three. However, if he built the company with the focus on what he could get out of it, he would probably have struggled to grow and build it so quickly. Instead, he built the company with the customer in mind and made them the core priority.

By making it all about the customer, he focused on how he could get to them to give his message, identified what they wanted and found the best people to delivery it. Throughout the growth of his events company, he made it about the customers, the service the speaker was giving and the marketing and promotion. During its growth, it was never about Daniel.

Lesson 4 - Identify current trends

As Daniel grew his business, he probably had a few ideas about what he was going to do when he first came to the UK. He was very quick to identify how the market was changing and was one of the early adopters of social media and the power of products to leverage your message.

This has formed the core part of his Key Person of Influence project. What Daniel did was recognize what was happening and create a service around it to meet the demand he anticipated. One of the core skills of an entrepreneur is to identify trends one, two or even three steps ahead of the market and take action. The KPI project is a perfect example of this.

Lesson 5 – Do not be restricted by geography

The new entrepreneur is no longer restricted by geography because the internet has allowed us access to a global local market. You are able to build a relationship with someone 5 miles away in the same way as with someone 5000 miles away. What this means is that more connections can be made through ideology than through geography.

If someone on the other side of the world wants to use your services because they have a better connection with you, they can. The benefit of this is you no longer have to compete on price. If what you have is of value and presented in the right way, anyone anywhere can buy your services or products.

DANIEL'S TOP TIPS

1. Don't watch the news.
2. Carry £500 on you at all times as a float.
3. Plan and take holidays.

David McQueen

> *'Vision without action is daydreaming and action without vision is a nightmare.'*
>
> Anon.

Since starting his own business at age 14, David McQueen has been passionate about business and storytelling. From tuckshops to event management, bookkeeping to IT support and personal development companies, he accounts his success to shaping a story that he, his team and his clients believe in.

David is a TV presenter and was the host of Pioneers TV and co-host for *'Vocation, Vocation, Vocation'*. As a trainer and coach he has designed and delivered programmes on leadership, presentation skills, career management and business development and has travelled all around the world as a conference and motivational speaker.

Five Lessons from David

Lesson 1 – Watch out for the signs, both literally and metaphorically

One of the excuses that people allow themselves to make, is that they don't have opportunities to do what they want to do. David talks about the day he walked down a street and saw a sign that said "Company Formation". For him, this was an actual sign to starting his journey metaphorically as well as in reality. What we need to do is not complain about our lack of opportunity but to instead look out for the signs around us that can inspire us to take action.

Lesson 2 – Get a mentor

Somebody who has been where you want to go can be a priceless commodity. Nobody can give you experience, yet you can learn from other people's experiences. There are several things you need to look out for when looking for a mentor: ensuring that you find somebody you can relate to, respect, like and above all, listen to. The value of a mentor can only really measured once you have experienced it. If you look at the most successful people in the world, they all have mentors of one type or another.

Lesson 3 – Become resourceful

When people start a business, the first things they look at are the resources they have. They may see that they are lacking in many parts and then give up, saying that it's too difficult or that they don't have the funds or time.

True entrepreneurial spirit is not related to how many resources you have what you do with what you do have. Become resourceful and you can start to attract resources.

Lesson 4 – Test and measure

We may think we know that what we have will sell and make millions, but there is no harm in testing and measuring. This is applicable not only for the physical product or service you may provide, but also for your marketing and branding. Carrying out surveys is a great way of getting market information. Your customers will tell you the truth. If you receive negative feedback, you can put it right, and if you receive positive comments, your customers will tell you and others, as we all like to be the bearer of good news.

Lesson 5 – Keep it simple

Don't make it complicated for people to engage with you. David talks about how Google entered the market by keeping it simple with a plain homepage that doesn't try to sell you anything or distract your attention. This lesson can be applied to any business – be clear and make it easy for the customer to interact with you. Keeping things simple also allows your customers to relate to you better, leading to greater loyalty.

DAVID'S TOP TIPS
1. Would people pay money for it? Is your idea commercially sound?
2. Get a mentor.
3. Believe in your capabilities.

I'm an Entrepreneur - Get Me Out of Here! The Lessons

Steve Clarke

> 'The best way to predict the future is to create it.'
> Pete Drucker

Steve has taken his own businesses from start-up to stock market flotation. He grew his last business to £30m in annual sales in just 8 years, sold out and retired at 45. He walks his talk. Everything he shares is from practical first hand experience – not hollow theory.

He has been privileged to speak to audiences all across Europe, the USA, the Middle East, South Africa, India and Australia – one common question crosses every geographical and cultural boundary... "How can we generate more leads, increase sales and profits...?"

That's precisely where he can help you. It's what makes his subject matter relevant, Steve makes it interesting, memorable and actionable. He shares performance enhancing ideas, helping people around the world put their sales performance on legal steroids and often (this part proves very popular) with less blood sweat and tears. www.eurekasales.co.uk

Five Lessons from Steve

Lesson 1 – Effort and focus

Steve left school at 16 with no qualifications, but being involved in his first business at 19 made him realise that income can come from two simple things, effort and focus.

A lot of emphasis is put on knowledge, skills and know-how when starting a business, but without tremendous effort and – more importantly – focus, nothing can be achieved. Effort isn't usually an issue, but you need to avoid being a busy fool and doing lots of stuff that doesn't actually get you what you want. Focus comes from knowing exactly what you want. You can become easily distracted if you don't have a clear end in mind.

Lesson 2 – Be open to opportunity

Without Steve being open to opportunity, his life would have taken a completely different turn. Steve believes in creating your own luck by being prepared when the opportunity presents itself and by taking action. People are often confronted with opportunities but they look around and decide that it's either not the right time, not the right conditions or that they'll do it when X happens. They are looking for the perfect conditions and the fact is, these perfect conditions never occur. It's about you becoming more resourceful with what you have and creating the conditions in which you can seize the opportunity. This is why, if you are prepared, luck will follow you.

Lesson 3 – Think outside of the box

We all know what this phrase means and can identify it when we see it. The problem is that we don't give ourselves the opportunity to think outside the box because of our existing behaviours and thought patterns. To be able to think outside the box, we have to challenge some of our absolute truths and assumptions. Steve needed to find a way to travel from the States and back, but had no money. He came up with a sponsorship deal with Continental, where he would be paid in flights. Perfect. Now if he hadn't challenged his assumptions that Continental would only consider a monetary transaction, the deal would never have been done.

Lesson 4 – Surround yourself with the right people

You can't do everything yourself. Most people who are entrepreneurial are very good at starting up, but not so hot on keeping it going, so this is where they need to get other people in. Initially this might not be possible, but it's important to think about what you need to do now so that when the time comes, you can get other people in to work in your business.

Lesson 5 – Commit fully

Are you prepared to FULLY commit? If there is any slight hesitation, you may struggle achieving all you want to as an entrepreneur. When you fully commit, things start to happen. The frustrating thing can be that they don't always happen in the way you expected them to. We may plan in our minds, but the universe has a funny way of making things happen. The moment you commit and step over the edge, amazing things start to happen. Are you prepared to take that step?

STEVE'S TOP TIPS

1. Be clear on your 'why'.
2. Be passionate.
3. Take action.

Chris Daems

> 'Formal education will make you a living;
> self-education will make you a fortune.'
>
> Jim Rohn

Chris Daems is the director of Principal Financial Solutions, a financial planning practice based in the city of London. During his career, Chris has worked for a number of large financial institutions before setting up his own business in 2009. Chris's clients range from high street fashion retailers employing thousands of individuals all the way to successful owner managed businesses.

In 2013 Chris reached the shortlist for 'Real Life Entrepreneur' and his business was the runner-up in 'Most Innovative Business' in the Federation of Small Business London Awards. So far in 2014 Chris has won two awards including the 'Unbiased pensions adviser of the year 2014'.

Five Lessons from Chris

Lesson 1 – Plan for the short-, medium- and long-term

When you start your business there is a tendency to only look at the short- and medium-terms, because if these can be sorted out, the long-term will look after itself. This maybe the case in some instances, but forward-planning can never be a bad thing.

A question to ask yourself in the pursuit of growing your business is, if I knew exactly what my long-term plan was, what decisions would I make today?

Lesson 2 – Start before you start

If you are in a job and planning to leave and set up your own business, you need to begin before you leave your job. There are so many things that you can start to do before launching your business full-time. Do some marketing, build your website and start telling people what you are doing.

Lesson 3 – Replace fear with fear

There will always be fear when you begin anything. The key here is to identify the fear you are feeling and then replace it with a fear that will produce productive behaviour. Chris talks about replacing the fear of doing something and failing with the fear of not doing it and having years of regret.

The key here is to identify what fear is going to motivate you in taking action that will produce some kind of result. Whatever the result, you will learn from it, so have nothing to lose!

Lesson 4 – Surround yourself with like-minded people

A great phrase that I am often quoting is that you are the average of the five people you associate with most. So if you want to up your average, you need to up the average of the people you hang out with.

By surrounding yourself with like-minded people, you give yourself a massive advantage in making decisions, taking calculated risks and avoiding the doubters that plague the world.

Lesson 5 – Big is not always better

Depending on what your business is, big is not always better. In today's world, you no longer need massive offices or big factories to be a success; a laptop, an idea and good relationships will do. Focus on quality and not quantity and people will come.

CHRIS'S TOP TIPS

1. Have a plan.
2. Meet people.
3. Use social media.

I'm an Entrepreneur - Get Me Out of Here! The Lessons

Thomas Power

> 'Success is walking from failure to failure with no loss of enthusiasm.'
>
> Winston Churchill

Thomas Power (50) is a networker, a matchmaker and a dealmaker who hunts constantly for new technology and business models that can improve business performance. He is the co-founder of Scredible which is in beta and will enable busy people to look good online.

Thomas is non-executive director of a number of companies, has published seven books and is an active public speaker. He is probably best known as the former chairman of social business network Ecademy, which was founded in 1998 with Penny Power and grew to 600,000 members. Thomas is married to Penny Power and they have three teenage children and two dogs.

Five Lessons from Thomas

Lesson 1 – Doubts: You never lose them but just get better at handling them

With the many different companies that Thomas has worked in, for and run, you would think that any self-doubt he may have would have long since diluted and disappeared. This isn't the case. What Thomas says is that he has just gotten better at handling it. So what can we learn from this? Well if you are doing what you want to do because of doubt and waiting for a time when the doubt will go away, you will be waiting for a very long time.

By doing something and taking action you learn to deal with the doubt better. But it never goes away. In fact what is evident is that the doubt, and the fear that comes with it, drives you to grow and prevents apathy.

Lesson 2 – Aim for small improvement every day

If you make just one small improvement every day, what impact would this have on your business? Thomas talks about Toyota's philosophy. They aim for a little improvement every day. This could be physical health, wellbeing, company, marriage, children or anything else. But these small, incremental improvements build up over time and can have a massive impact on your life.

Lesson 3 – Hit a target others can't see

Being an entrepreneur is about doing what other won't. This can mean seeing a market that others have not either identified or cannot see. Trusting your gut instincts or your intuition can be crucial here.

Lesson 4 – Build a community

Without people there are no businesses. Thomas's assertion is that there can be no business without building some sort of community around your brand/product/service. Building a community means building your social capital, which then gives you the ability to get things done. The lesson here is that by building a community, you are in effect becoming a magnet and attracting customer, supplies, shareholders and employees.

Lesson 5 – Don't judge anyone

One clear message Thomas has for running your own business is to never judge anyone. You never know who is 'packing your parachute', to use the metaphor he memorably uses. You simply never know to whom you are talking.

Further lessons include having the courage of your convictions, being prepared to fail, eating the right things to have enough energy, not being afraid and building communities.

THOMAS'S TOP TIPS

1. Build a big network.
2. Whatever capital you think you need, multiply it by a factor of ten.
3. Be patient with yourself.

Suraj Sodha

> 'In order to succeed, your desire for success should be greater than your fear of failure.'
> Bill Cosby

Suraj Sodha is an in-demand international speaker and internet entrepreneur from London, England, with ambitious ideas and results-oriented solutions to start and grow businesses online.

Suraj is known for his extremely focused expertise and access to a respected network of entrepreneurs and marketers around the world.

Suraj helps businesses and entrepreneurs create content for their blogs and YouTube channel.

Five Lessons from Suraj

Lesson 1 – You can choose when you work

One thing that society conditions us into is the 9-5 ethic. We school between 9-3, to university or college and have lectures during the day, then go to work and work 9-5. We get conditioned to work these hours and the other hours are seen as leisure hours. Being an entrepreneur you can work whatever hours you want.

This does not mean that you work less, but just when you choose to. When you first start out running your own business, you usually find yourself working longer hours and at so-called 'unsociable' times. The crucial difference is that you are doing what you love, which means that the long hours do not feel that long. It doesn't feel like work at all.

Lesson 2 – Success leaves clues

We have a habit of ignoring what we already know or dismissing small achievements that make a big difference. When Suraj was deciding on what to do after leaving the corporate world, he became overwhelmed with all the information around him.

So he looked at his background and in particular where he already had a little knowledge and some success. For him, this was the Internet and blogging. Success leaves clues. Have a look at the little successes you have had in your past and think about the clues they have left for you to build on.

Lesson 3 - Do what you love

Do what you love and you will never have to work again in your life. Being an entrepreneur can be a thankless task, so doing something that you do not love is double torture. Circumstances, responsibilities and the environment may not be conducive to doing what you love. All I would say is no, it is not easy, but it is possible.

Suraj had a successful career in the corporate law world in the palm of his hand, but he knew that he would not be happy or have the lifestyle he craved. Be brave, take action and create the life you deserve.

Lesson 4 - Keep it simple

Keep it simple in two ways, both in the way you run your business and in what you offer your customers. In some cases you find that a business or industry uses a lot of unnecessary jargon and industry specific words. People fall into the trap of thinking they need to use this jargon to look like an expert and as if they know what they are talking about.

Keep it simple for you customers to understand and engage with you and your business will be simple to run.

Lesson 5 - Model the best

Like having a mentor, modelling can fast-track you to success. Find someone who is doing what you want to do. But not just anyone – find the best and model them.

When you model the best, do not judge. Don't say, "Well I'm not like that." The key is to get out of your own way, trust the process, model what the best do and you will not be far off being modelled yourself one day.

SURAJ'S TOP TIPS

1. Have passion for what you do.
2. Build a mailing list.
3. Sell it before you make it.

Vicki Wusche

> *'If you think you're too small to have an impact, try going to bed with a mosquito.'*
> Anita Roddick

Vicki Wusche is a vibrant and engaging property and business entrepreneur. In 2013 she was recommended by the Telegraph as one of the UK's top 25 most influential people in property.

Vicki has published three books: *'Using Other People's Money – How to Invest in Property'*, *'Make More Money From Property; from investor thinking to a business mind-set'* and *'Property for the next generation; preparing your family for a wealth future'*. She is now working on a fourth book and the third edition of *'Using Other People's Money'*.

Vicki speaks to entrepreneurs, young people, business owners, investors and employees, inspiring her audiences to understand that 'it' is possible. Her two businesses, The Sourcer Apprentice and The Property Sourcers keep her occupied in between her holidays scuba diving all over the world.

Five Lessons from Vicki

Lesson 1 – What are your values?

You know what you know; you don't know what you don't know. Vicki found herself in the position of knowing exactly what she wanted from life until shit a fracture point - in her case, redundancy. This allowed her to look more deeply at her values and after attending a seminar, her whole thinking changed. Bearing in mind that she had been a university lecturer teaching business and entrepreneurial skills, this was astonishing. The key point that came out from this was an understanding of her core values. The lesson we can take from this is that if you are unsure of what to do, you need to find your values, your 'why'.

Lesson 2 – Take responsibility for your life

This may seem obvious, but in our current society, it is very easy to simply 'float', subconsciously wait for things to happen to you and then react, instead of taking responsibility for your life and actively make things happen.

So what does this look like? Well it could be something as simple as making that phone call, doing your research and acting on it, talking to people who are already in the industry or going to a seminar to learn new techniques or gain a different perspective. Anything that means you are doing something positive to make change happen.

Lesson 3 - Create wealth, not money

The obvious surface reason for starting a business is to make lots of money. Whilst there is nothing wrong with that, money is in fact just a barometer of how much value you are giving or how successful you are. If you instead focus on creating wealth, as Vicki said, you are more concerned about what you do with the money and how much freedom you can create. Wealth is also about making assets that will constantly be putting money back into your business. If you generate lots of money without creating the time to enjoying it, there's not much point in running the business at all.

Lesson 4 - Think on a different level

When you begin making changes to your life, you will inevitably start to think about things differently. Changing your thinking before you make those changes is a key to easing the transition and can avoid you becoming overwhelmed with fear, doubt, low confidence and ultimately failure. So how do you change your thinking? Start to hang around and associate with people who are going to change your thinking, go to events, seminars and networking events and be open to new ideas and approaches.

Lesson 5 - Get technical knowledge

A lot of Vicki's lessons and tips are based on what you can do to change your thinking, behaviour and actions, and rightly so; it is these skills that make or break a business. What is also important is to understand the technical side of things. Don't be left short in the area you are focusing on by lacking the technical knowhow. Vicki chose property as a vehicle for wealth creation and once she understood what she wanted and how it could be done, made sure that she got the right technical knowhow to do it herself.

VICKI'S TOP TIPS

1. Change your thinking.
2. Know your 'why'.
3. Do the numbers.

Simon Jordan

> *'An entrepreneur tends to bite off a little more than he can chew, hoping he'll quickly learn how to chew it.'*
>
> Roy Ash

Simon Jordan is a marketing and branding strategist, coach and also the International Amazon 5-star-rated author of '*How to Sky RocketYour Business (without burning your fingers)*'.

He's an international speaker offering business and marketing advice with a good portion of motivation and inspiration thrown in. He is also a marketing mentor to thousands of business owners worldwide via his mentoring groups, TV and radio shows.

Five Lessons from Simon

Lesson 1 – Understand your place in the market

It doesn't matter what you have done - you may have to start at zero. One thing that we learn from Simon's journey is that it doesn't matter who he has worked with or how successful he has been; he is always open to new ideas and doing the dirty work. Simon has a very good reputation within the corporate market, but knew that this would mean nothing within the SME market, where he wanted to build his business. He knew that he had to build his reputation from the ground up and he didn't let his ego get the better of him. Instead, he rolled his sleeves up and in his own words "even went to the opening of an envelope" to get himself known.

Lesson 2 – Be consistent

When Simon went to events, he realised that there was no pattern to what he did but understood that people like consistency and certainty. He therefore wanted to create a brand that was professional and open, hence his look of a pinstripe suit with an open collar. Wherever you see Simon in a professional capacity, you will see him wearing the same thing. This ensures that people 'get' what he is about and he is able to create an image.

Lesson 3 – Four must-haves

Belief – without this it's like pushing an elephant uphill.

Faith – in your own abilities and belief that you will get the business.

Guts – never, ever give up. You will get knockbacks, but you have to believe and keep going. Many an entrepreneur has given up just before everything would have fallen into place.

Action – without doing something, nothing will happen. People often don't take action because they're not ready or it's not the right time or the weather is not right. The message here is to just do something.

Lesson 4 – Get the marketing right

Many people start a business because they are good at what they do, e.g. being the technician. Simon uses the example of a massage therapist. They may be the best massage therapist in the world, but if they don't know how to market themselves or the business, they will struggle. Many a frustrated business fails because of lack of marketing and sales, rather than because of how good they are at what they do or provide.

Lesson 5 – Have confidence in your own ability

Be confident in what you do. If you do not have confidence in yourself no one else will. There will be times when things just don't work. Whatever happens never lose your own confidence in your ability. If you do, remind of yourself of all the things you have achieved, especially the ability to start your own business.

SIMON'S TOP TIPS

1. Do your research - is there a need for your product/service in the marketplace?
2. What are the benefits you're offering the market?
3. Don't worry about your logo.

Sue Richardson

'A bird doesn't sing because it has an answer; it sings because it has a song.'

Maya Angelou

Sue Richardson has 20 years' experience in publishing, having spent several years as a freelance editor before moving on to become a publisher in 2000. She is passionate about books and believes that when well-conceived and produced they have the potential to change the world. Sue is Managing Director of Sue Richardson Associates Ltd, an independent publishing consultancy dedicated to guiding and supporting budding authors on their publishing journey.

Five Lessons from Sue

Lesson 1 – It doesn't matter about your background

Sue's story is fascinating. She hasn't had the typical journey of a would-be entrepreneur. In some aspects it happened by accident. But what is evident is that she developed into a businesswoman, not in spite of her background but because of it. What she identified was that she is very good at what she does and she has built her business around this.

This demonstrates that it doesn't matter what you have done. As long as you are good at what you do and are prepared to work at it, you can make it.

Lesson 2 – Adapt to the market

Sue created the *'Textile Directory'* after discovering that the market needed it. However, after some years it became evident that the purpose of the directory had become obsolete due to the internet. Whatever business you are in, you need to adapt to the market conditions. Just look at what happened to Woolworth's.

Lesson 3 – Niche

Know what you're good at and be good at what you know. If you are able to niche, you immediately stand out from the crowd, elevate yourself about the noise and give yourself an opportunity to have a voice.

Narrowing your market by niching can expand your market rather that reduce it. This is because you can them command greater fees, be seen as an expert and reduce your competition.

Lesson 4 – Write a book

It doesn't matter what business you are in, a book can open up doors for you. Many of the entrepreneurs featured here have either written or featured in books, like in this one!

Lesson 5 – Tell your story

Everyone journey has a message. People want to hear your story. By telling your story you will inspire others and be inspired yourself. We often underestimate what we have done and not until it is written down does it become evident just what we have achieved and what we can do.

SUE'S TOP TIPS
1. Tell your story.
2. Surround yourself with the right people.
3. Get out of your BED - Blame, Excuse and Denial - and paddle your OARs - Ownership, Accountability and Responsibility.

I'm an Entrepreneur - Get Me Out of Here! The Lessons

Penny Power

> *'My philosophy is that not only are you responsible for your life, but doing the best at this moment puts you in the best place for the next moment.'*
>
> Oprah Winfrey

Penny joined the Technology Sector in 1983 and built many sales channels and help people that find technology challenging.

In 1998 Penny and Thomas Power founded Ecademy, the UK's first social network for business. Ecademy was sold in 2012.

In 2010 Penny authored a bestselling book, '*Know Me, Like Me, Follow Me*' and also the Digital Business Britain Manifesto supported by The Department of Business, Innovation and Skills.

In 2011, Penny founded the Digital Youth Academy bringing a new Apprenticeship to market to help young people get jobs that played to their Born Digital strengths.

In 2014 Penny started working with Scredible, a USA software company that provides a powerful solution for individuals and companies to develop their online identity.

In the 2014 New Years Honours List Penny was awarded an OBE for her commitment to Entrepreneurship and Social Digital Development.

Five Lessons from Penny

Lesson 1 – It's about relationships

Littered throughout Penny's journey is the importance she places on relationships. When she was working in the corporate world where it was all about the transactions, she had one moment where she showed a little bit of care and as a result got one of her biggest sales.

Ecademy was founded upon the concept that relationships can be built to benefit all aspects of our lives, including both social and business.

Lesson 2 – It's about values

The natural progression to this is being true to your values. When starting and building a business, it is natural to look at the 'what' and 'how' of making money. What Penny is big on is being true to her values and the values of the people she connects with. When you are building your business with your values in mind, it provides a better foundation upon which to grow. Values are the bricks and mortar to your business. If you are true to them and use them as a base, in times of adversity you will have a solid foundation to build from again.

Lesson 3 – Be an evangelist; shift minds

If you are going to take the huge decision to start a business and be an entrepreneur, you have to be evangelical in your business. If you are not shouting from the rooftops about your business, no one else will.

The lesson here is that if you want to shift minds and get people to understand your values, you need to tell people about it and not hold back. This will attract people who hold the same values as you, exactly the kind of people you want and need to build relationships and do business with.

Lesson 4 – Build your social capital

We understand the phrase 'financial capital' and life without social capital wouldn't be possible. When you build your business, nothing happens without people. 'Social capital' is the phrase given to the capital you build around trust, goodwill, influence and emotional support.

When social capital is present and built upon, everything becomes that much easier.

Lesson 5 – Intent

What is your intent in starting a business? To say "make money" is easy and rather shallow. Money can sometimes be seen as the barometer of your success, but intent is communicating the real reason you do what you do for yourself and your clients. When this happens, it all starts to flow.

PENNY'S TOP TIPS

1. Build your social capital.
2. Get your answers from the heart. This is where your customers listen from.
3. Have tenacity and lots of it!

I'm an Entrepreneur - Get Me Out of Here! The Lessons

Brad Burton

> *'Regardless of who you are or what you have been, you can be what you want to be.'*
>
> W. Clement Stone

From a humble start in Manchester to MD of 4Networking, the fastest-growing social business network in the UK, Brad Burton is the UK's No 1 motivational speaker and bestselling author of the highest-rated business book on Amazon, *'Get Off Your Arse'* and its sequel, *'Get Off Your Arse Too'*.

Six years ago Brad was delivering pizzas to keep his start-up business afloat. He used the incentive of £25k personal debt to build a multi-million pound business network and now he is delivering inspirational, hilarious and provocative speaking events on life, business and motivation.

Don't let the jeans and t-shirt fool you....

Five Lessons from Brad

Lesson 1 – One moment can make the difference

We all get moments where we look back and think, 'That was the moment when everything changed'. The penny drops. Allow a moment to be inspired to take action and create the life you want.

Lesson 2 – Pride keeps you where you're at

Your own pride can prevent you from moving forward. Brad had to admit to himself and his to his family that things were not working out and had to swallow his pride and do something about it. Don't let past fears and pride get in the way of making a difference today.

Lesson 3 – Just start

One thing that Brad is big on is just starting. Yes, you can plan, research and all that stuff, but unless you start and get your hands dirty you will never make a business. We may have an idea of how something will work and be successful, yet there is plenty of evidence to suggest that by starting something, the results you want may come from an unintended source.

Lesson 4 – Play full-out

One of the main reasons many startups fail is that they do not play full-out. The lesson here is that if you are going to start a business, you might as well really go for it. Play full-out and get rid of the safety nets.

Having no safety net means that you have no choice but to play full-out and are therefore more likely to succeed. Related to this is not waiting for the perfect conditions. There will never be the perfect conditions.

Lesson 5 – Never judge

Brad is very big on being his own man; he doesn't wear flashy suits or talk in a posh accent. He wears a T-shirt and jeans wherever he is. We have preconceived ideas about people, depending on how they dress, talk, what school they went to and their social up-bringing. Yet when you first meet someone, you never really know who you're speaking to. So don't judge but be open and treat everybody you meet equally. Difficult but not impossible.

BRAD'S TOP TIPS
1. Be the market leader.
2. Make money in the real world, not on spreadsheets.
3. Hit the ground running.

Section 3

Conclusion

So can you do it?

Can you be an entrepreneur, start your own business, and live the life you want? One thing that is evident from reading the challenges, lessons and success of all the entrepreneurs in this book is that there isn't just one way. There isn't a blueprint that you can follow to become an 'entrepreneur'.

One thing that this process has taught me is that anything is possible if you put your mind to it. Not one of these entrepreneurs had or has it easy. Some started young, some later in life. Some had to sell their houses, others left high paid corporate jobs. What is consistent is that they all made decisions and acted upon them.

This is the first stage; make a decision then act upon it. The second part is, will you do this acting as a professional amateur or as a true professional?

What's the difference? A professional amateur will have all the intentions of starting and running a business, but during the process become overpowered by these behaviours and thoughts: procrastination; delaying making that call; planning too much; being hesitant; coming up with reasons for not being ready and confusing opinion with fact.

So does the professional have these thoughts and behaviours? Yes they do, but they don't let them affect what is going to happen. After all, the main reason for these thoughts and behaviours is fear. The professional recognises it as just fear yet does it anyway. To get to where they are now, our entrepreneurs all acted professionally.

In his book *'Turning Pro'*, Steven Pressfield talks about what makes us turn pro. He says it's a conscious decision and that the moment is accompanied by powerful drama and emotion. All the people in this book remember clear moments when they made a decision which was followed by massive action driven by an emotional connection. This is not to say that people who work for someone else aren't professional. When you turn pro, you start to behave in a way where you have complete respect for yourself, don't come up with excuses and stop procrastinating, knowing that you are only answerable to yourself.

One characteristic that stands out from these interviews is that every one of the entrepreneurs is prepared to defer gratification. What does this mean? It means to forgo a reward now. To invest in ourselves, week after week, month after month, and sometimes year after year, to reap the rewards later, however these rewards choose to show up.

When you make that decision, your mind changes. Your thinking changes. It is often cited that the mindset needed for a job is very different to the mindset required when you are running your own business. The leader in a corporate world leads with a different intent than the leader running their own business.

This is why the transition can be so painful, but life teaches you how to handle this. It's certainly not something you learn in school. The difference here is that when you make that transition there is no turning back. You become unemployable. Your standards change, your expectations change, your tolerance changes. For a period of time your become your business, your vision and your mission. This is difficult for someone who has worked for someone else all their lives and has no desire to start their own business to understand.

Not one of the 55 lessons or 33 tips highlighted in this book are learnt in school. Not one tip is 'Get a degree' or 'Get 10 GCSEs'; they are all things that come from within. What does this tell us? Well what it does say is that there are no real barriers, only those that we put up ourselves. Of course depending on what you want to do there might be financial barriers or resources, but as quite a few have said, it's not about what you have or don't have but about what you do with what you do have, i.e. how resourceful you can be.

We allow the immediately obvious things that seem impossible to stop us from even making a start. Brad Burton says, "Just start," Simon Jordan, "Get on with it," Steve Clarke, "Be open to opportunity," andn Suraj even says "Sell it before you make it." Radical. With the advent of the internet age, we are no longer restricted by location and our own geography.

Essentially the only reason we do not start is because we do not want to fail. Nothing else. If you knew for certain that you were going to succeed, nothing would stop you because you know that the risk will pay off. You hear stories of highly successful people who have been through bankruptcies, have lost their house and are down to the last pound in their pocket. It might make you feel as though you *have* to have a major failure before you can be successful.

Failure should not be avoided, just accepted. It will happen. The scale will depend on what you want. What you need to focus on is how you react to it. By avoiding the risk of failure you hold something back and don't play full-out, a lesson that a few of our entrepreneurs have stressed.

Some would say that starting a business is relatively easy, but that keeping it going and growing is the tough part. This is partly because when you first start out, you are full of passion and enthusiasm and some would say this carries you for the first few months, but then reality kicks home and you feel overworked without seeing any reward. This is when, as some of the entrepreneurs have indicated, you need to know your 'why'. What is the big picture for you?

So can you really do it? In an word, yes, but you need to be patient. This book contains many lessons from different people at different periods of their life. But now what? You've read this book and heard the stories, but what's next? All the advice in the world means nothing unless you do something and take action. Taking action is the only thing you can do to ensure that the lessons you have read in this book really make a difference to your life.

Here is a 5-point plan of what you can do now. If you follow through on these 5 points you will be far ahead of the curve.

1. Know your 'why', both for yourself and for when you call one of the entrepreneurs. If you have clarity about what you want to do and what you want to talk to them about, they are more likely to want to talk to you.

2. Pick three of the entrepreneurs in this book and contact them. Yes contact them. Sometimes there is a perception that they are incredibly busy and wouldn't

want to talk to you. But ask yourself this question: How did Baiju get them to be part of this book? Answer: I asked them. What I also did is tell them why. I gave them the big picture about this book to create a win-win situation. This brings me onto point two.

3. Make a decision. Depending on what stage you are in your life, this decision will differ and you will likely be:

   a. In a job you like, but wanting to do your own thing. Decision to make: Do you want to start it now or do you have the patience to wait? If you like what you do, it might be sensible to build up capital and then leave on your own terms to start your business.

   b. In a job you don't like and wanting to start a business. This is the most common scenario. The key here is to make a decision to leave, but not to leave until you have a few ducks in line. When I left my job, I made the decision 18 months before I actually left. I knew I had to get my finances in order, get a website done and understand my market better before I actually made the jump. You sometimes get away with it, like Brad Burton, but even he advises having some sort of plan in place before making the move.

   c. Started a business but things are not going well. What you need to do is to stop and reflect. One reason for your business not doing well is that you might be overwhelmed with all that you have to do and end up doing nothing, becoming a busy fool and thus not growing your business. The decision to make is to take lots of small steps. Each day ask yourself, "What one small thing can I do that will move me towards where I want to go?"

d. Started a business and all is going well. Never rest on your laurels. Keep learning, keep up to date with what's happening in the world to help you grow your business

4. Become the go-to person in your industry. Whatever you do and aim to do, whether it is service- or product-related, become the authority in what you do and your credibility will be enhanced.

5. Read this book every 6 weeks. We all have moments when we doubt, feel low and lack confidence. Reading this book, or any other book that contains inspiring stories, will remind you of how good you are and that you have all you need to create the success you want.

I hope that you have enjoyed this book and that this is the start or the continuation of your journey into entrepreneurship. Remember that it is never too late. I was employed until the age of 37 and many of the entrepreneurs in this book started later on in their lives. In some cases this is not a bad place to start, having some corporate experience behind you. You bring different things to the party.

Don't let anything about your past stop you pursuing your dreams and goals. Whatever your background, experience, age, sex or vision, you can do it. The world needs you to step up.

Summary of Lessons

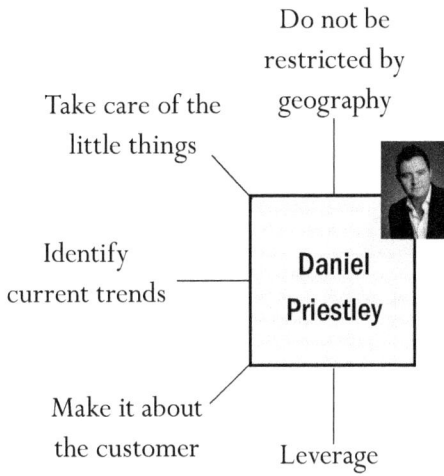

Take care of the little things

Do not be restricted by geography

Identify current trends

Daniel Priestley

Make it about the customer

Leverage

Top Tips

1. Don't watch the news.
2. Carry £500 on you at all times as a float.
3. Plan and take holidays.

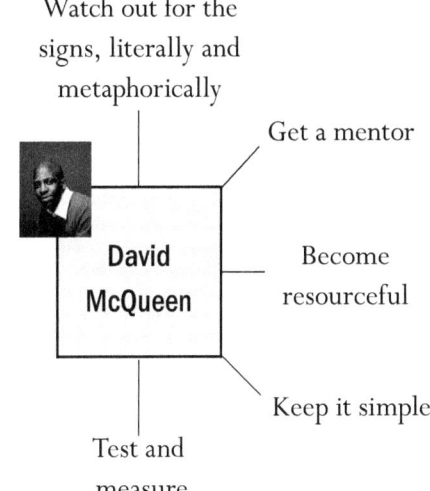

Top Tips

1. Make sure your idea is commercially viable.
2. Get a mentor.
3. Believe in your capabilities.

Watch out for the signs, literally and metaphorically

Get a mentor

David McQueen

Become resourceful

Test and measure

Keep it simple

Summary of Lessons (cont.)

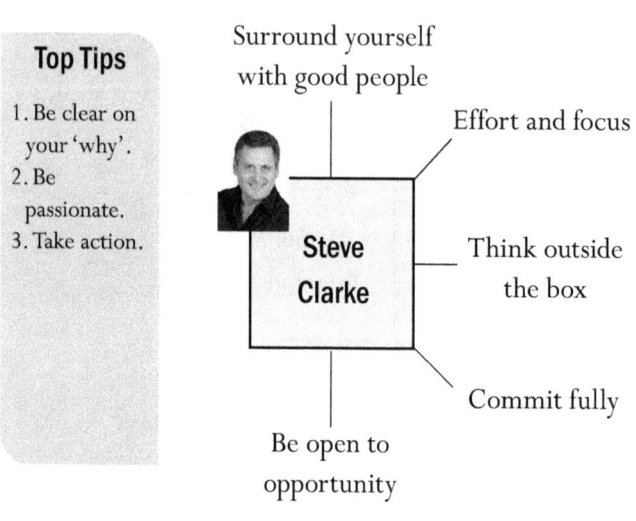

Top Tips
1. Be clear on your 'why'.
2. Be passionate.
3. Take action.

Steve Clarke
- Surround yourself with good people
- Effort and focus
- Think outside the box
- Commit fully
- Be open to opportunity

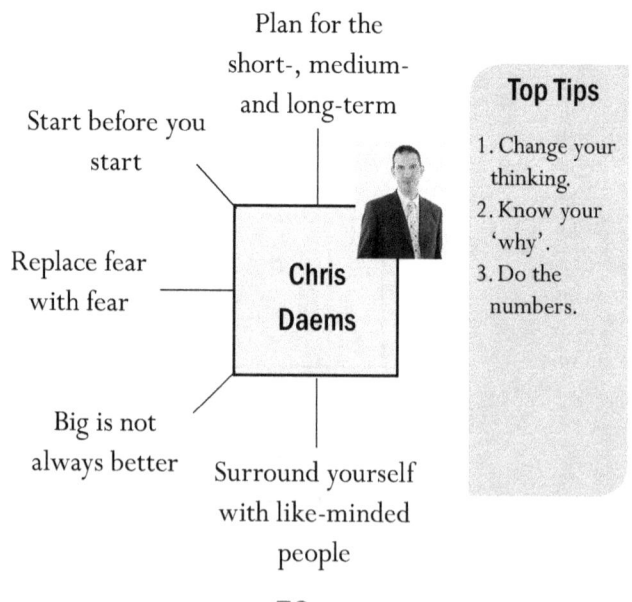

Chris Daems
- Start before you start
- Plan for the short-, medium- and long-term
- Replace fear with fear
- Big is not always better
- Surround yourself with like-minded people

Top Tips
1. Change your thinking.
2. Know your 'why'.
3. Do the numbers.

Summary of Lessons (cont.)

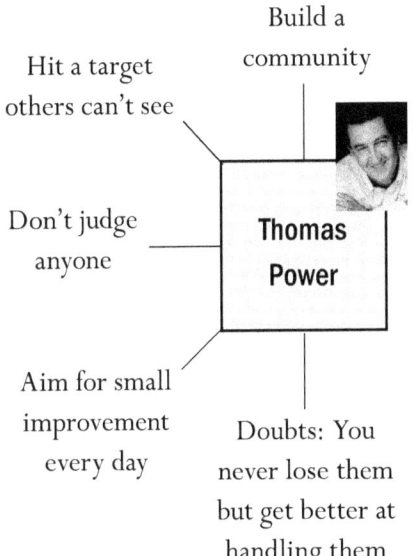

Thomas Power

- Hit a target others can't see
- Build a community
- Don't judge anyone
- Aim for small improvement every day
- Doubts: You never lose them but get better at handling them

Top Tips
1. Build a big network.
2. Whatever capital you think you'll need, multiply it by a factor of ten.
3. Be patient with yourself.

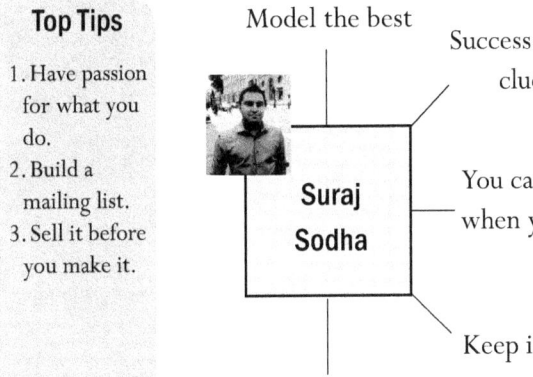

Suraj Sodha

- Model the best
- Success leaves clues
- You can choose when you work
- Keep it simple
- Do what you love

Top Tips
1. Have passion for what you do.
2. Build a mailing list.
3. Sell it before you make it.

Summary of Lessons (cont.)

Top Tips
1. Change your thinking.
2. Know your 'why'.
3. Do the numbers.

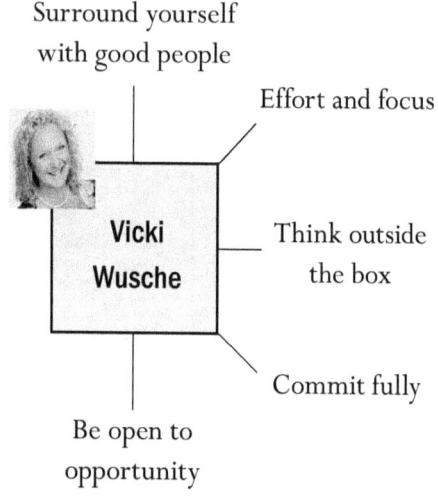

Vicki Wusche

- Surround yourself with good people
- Effort and focus
- Think outside the box
- Commit fully
- Be open to opportunity

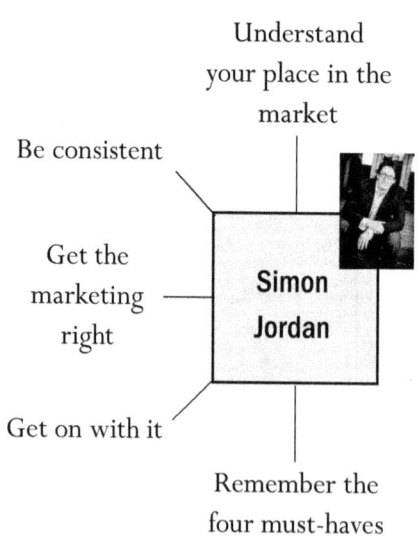

Simon Jordan

- Understand your place in the market
- Be consistent
- Get the marketing right
- Get on with it
- Remember the four must-haves

Top Tips
1. Do your research - is there a need for your product/service?
2. What benefits are you offering the market?
3. Don't worry about your logo.

Summary of Lessons (cont.)

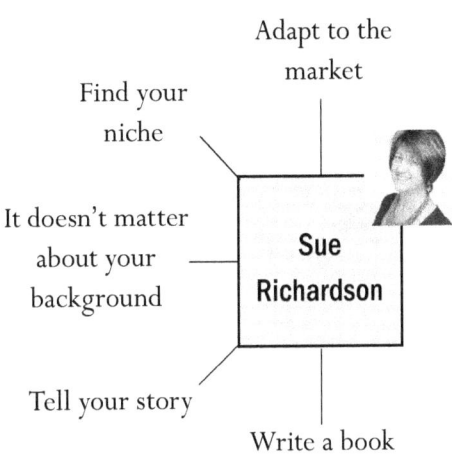

- Find your niche
- Adapt to the market
- It doesn't matter about your background
- **Sue Richardson**
- Tell your story
- Write a book

Top Tips
1. Tell your story.
2. Surround yourself with the right people.
3. Get out of your BED and paddle your OARs.

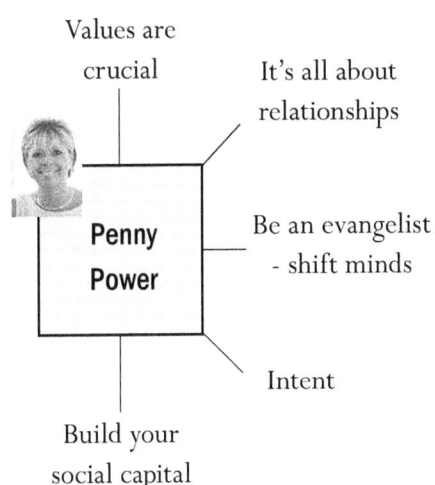

Top Tips
1. Build your social capital.
2. Get your answers from the heart. This is where your customers listen from.
3. Have tenacity and lots of it!

- Values are crucial
- It's all about relationships
- **Penny Power**
- Be an evangelist - shift minds
- Intent
- Build your social capital

Summary of Lessons (cont.)

Top Tips
1. Be the market leader.
2. Make money in the real world, not on spreadsheets.
3. Hit the ground running.

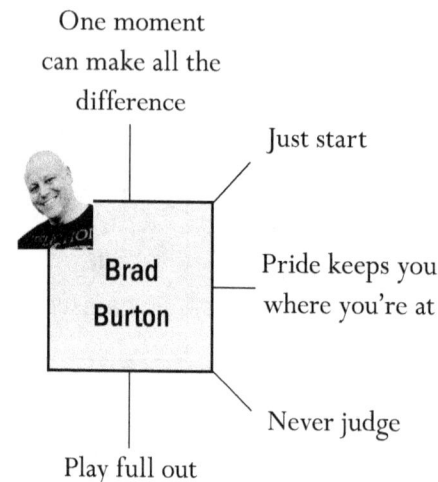

Brad Burton

- One moment can make all the difference
- Just start
- Pride keeps you where you're at
- Never judge
- Play full out

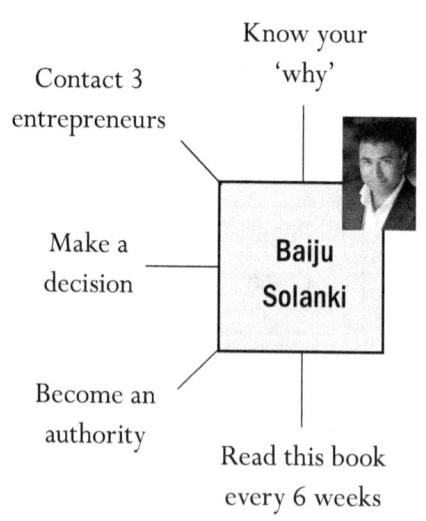

Baiju Solanki

- Contact 3 entrepreneurs
- Know your 'why'
- Make a decision
- Become an authority
- Read this book every 6 weeks

Top Tips
1. Don't let fear hold you back.
2. Believe in your impossible.
3. Be open to opportunity.

About the Author

Baiju Solanki is a Speaker, Author and Performance Coach. With a background in Psychology and Sales, he specialises in working with small business owners and corporates to grow their sales, inspire their teams and develop behaviours that sustain success. A sought-after speaker and trainer, Baiju is enthusiastic about entrepreneurship and inspiring people to achieve their potential.

To find out more about Baiju and how you or your company can grow and prosper in these tough times, visit his website at www.baijusolanki.com, or send him a tweet at @baijusolanki.

I'm An Entrepreneur Community

What now? Come join the I'm An Entrepreneur community, be inspired, share ideas and gain insights with like-minded individuals.

Join the community at : www.ImAnEntrepreneur.Biz

Facebook: www.facebook.com/ImAnEntrepreneurGetMeOutofHere

Twitter: use #ImAnEntrepreneur to tell us about your business! @WannaBeEnt

LinkedIn group: www.linkedin.com/groups/Im-Entrepreneur-Meet-up

For updates and news on I'm An Entrepreneur events, visit www.baijusolanki.com.

I'm an Entrepreneur - Get Me Out of Here! The Lessons

www.ingramcontent.com/pod-product-compliance
Lightning Source LLC
Chambersburg PA
CBHW071757170526
45167CB00003B/1073